TRY

A PLAY ABOUT LOVE, LIFE AND OCD

RICK WOOD

© Copyright Rick Wood 2016

Cover by James at GoOnWrite.com

No part of this book may be reproduced without the author's express permission.

Any likeness to real person is entirely coincidental.

For information on rights to perform this play, email
rickwoodwriter@yahoo.com

SCENE 1

The calendar to the side of the stage is set to '2013'. The stage is laid out with a bed on one side, and a table with two chairs on the other.

Holly and Kyle storm into their bedroom, Kyle following Holly who is clearly angry.

KYLE
   Are you angry?

HOLLY
   No.

KYLE
   Are you sure you are not angry?

. . .

HOLLY
Yes.

KYLE
What, yes as in you are angry, or yes as in you are sure you're not angry?

Holly grows confused, and hurriedly tidies the room.

HOLLY
Well, I – whichever one means I'm fine. I'm fine.

KYLE
Now I know what that means.

HOLLY
What?

KYLE
Fine. That doesn't mean you're fine, that means you're pissed off.

HOLLY
Don't try to psychoanalyse me, Kyle.

KYLE

I'm not, Holly – Holly –

Kyle rushes in front of Holly and stops her, placing his hands on her arms. He looks her deep in the eye.

KYLE
Would you please just tell me what is wrong? I feel like I'm supposed to guess.

HOLLY
You're supposed to just know, Kyle, you did, so you should know.

KYLE
Yes, that's all very well in a perfect world where I'm a mind reader – but I am not. I have no idea. But I would very much like to fix it. So, Holly, just tell me.

Holly hesitates.

HOLLY
You said Teresa's hat was nice.

KYLE
… That's it?

. . .

HOLLY

You didn't say that about my hat. You think I look stupid in a hat. You think Teresa looks amazing, you think I look stupid, so you may as well just run off with her.

Kyle laughs.

KYLE

Really, Holly, is that all it is?

Holly turns furious again, and continues to storm around the room, angrily cleaning.

KYLE

Aw come on Holly, that is ridiculous.

HOLLY

I am not ridiculous!

KYLE

That's not what I said.

HOLLY

Look – I know I'm irrational and I know I'm crazy, but I don't want you to tell me I'm crazy, I just want you to tell me I look better in a hat than Teresa, but I don't want to have to put those words in your mouth because you should just think of it yourself, because now I've told you to say it, it will sound ingenuine.

KYLE

Okay, I won't say it then.

HOLLY

Urgh, why not!

Holly storms off stage (into the bathroom.) Kyle stands outside the bathroom.

KYLE

Okay, Holly, I'm sorry. I'm sorry. I should have said that whilst she looks nice, you look nicer, and there is no way she can match up to you.

HOLLY

(off stage) So you still think she looks nice?

KYLE

No! Yes! I – I don't know. Why does this matter? You look amazing Holly, far more amazing than her.

The toilet flushes and Holly re-enters.

. . .

HOLLY
Really?

KYLE
Yes, of course.

HOLLY
Do you really think she looks silly in a hat? Were you just saying that to be polite?

KYLE
Of course, Holly, you know no one even comes close to you. You could wear, like, a mickey mouse hat, and still make it look stunning. The hat doesn't maketh the woman, the woman maketh the hat.

Holly sighs, smiles and gives him a big hug. There is a long pause.

HOLLY
What about her dress?

KYLE
Yeah, that was quite nice, purple suited her.

Holly quickly pulls away and hits him.

. . .

HOLLY
>I was wearing purple!

She storms off.

KYLE
>Oh come on!

He goes to exit after her, but she has slammed the door. He turns around and sits down, burying his head in his arms.

Holly slowly re-enters the stage, looking regretfully solemn.

HOLLY
>I'm sorry.

KYLE
>It's okay.

HOLLY
>No, I am. Really.

KYLE
>I knew what the deal was, I knew what I was getting into.

. . .

HOLLY
But you shouldn't have to -

KYLE
But I do.

Kyle turns and puts his arms around her.

HOLLY
I wish I didn't have to.... Sometimes, it just feels like I should have a medal for going out in the first place. You can leave. I mean, if you want to. I understand. I wouldn't stay.

KYLE
Yes you would.

HOLLY
Would I?

KYLE
You are a good person.

HOLLY
I'm an attractive person. Doesn't make me a good person.

KYLE

Oh, I don't know.... It kinda makes up for some of it.

He smiles and forces a laugh from her.

HOLLY
Maybe I should go back on them. Make me more tolerable. Would you like that? Would you prefer me on pills?

Kyle lets go of her, turns around, and lets out a big sigh.

KYLE
I –

He hesitates.

HOLLY
You would.

KYLE
No, that's not what it is.

HOLLY
You're leaving me.

KYLE

No! For god sake, no.

He turns and looks at her.

KYLE
I don't see a woman who is depressed, or bipolar, or.... mental. What makes it worse is that you seem adamant that I will leave you because of it.

HOLLY
You will leave me.

Long silence.

KYLE
You really think I'm that fickle?

HOLLY
I just think I'm that bad.

KYLE
Maybe you just don't know me at all.

HOLLY
Maybe you haven't seen my worst yet. It's a nice thought, Kyle. But practically...

She shakes her head.

HOLLY

Wait until my arm is dripping with blood. Wait until I've punched you for helping. Wait until I've driven every bit of good will out of you, spent all our money, driven our car into the wall, then laid in bed and blamed you for everything. Wait until the Doctors still can't help me. Would you stay, then?

He looks to the floor.

HOLLY

Would you stay, knowing that I won't get better?

KYLE

You will get better.

She forces an ingenuine smile. There is a long pause, as they just look at each other.

She turns and leaves.

Exit.

SCENE 2

Kyle changes the calendar to 2015. Kyle sits at the table, solemnly, a glass of whiskey in front of him. He looks devastated.

His phone rings.

He ignores it and takes a sip of his drink.

He waits a few more moments, then answers the phone.

KYLE
Hello? … No, we're planning on taking the casket straight to the funeral home, they said they didn't need to do an autopsy.... It was obvious. I – Sorry, I need to go.... No, look, all the information will be sent out.... Please, I need to go -

. . .

He hurriedly hangs up, stands, and walks to the opposite side of the stage.

Holly enters cheerfully, changing the calendar to 2010.

A cafe. Holly sits at a table reading a book.

Kyle instantly becomes happier and walks over to her.

KYLE
This is where we first met.

HOLLY
I noticed your eyes.

KYLE
I noticed your smile.

HOLLY
I noticed your hair.

KYLE
I noticed your tits.

They both laugh. Kyle sits opposite her enthusiastically.

. . .

KYLE

Is that Airman's book on the psychology of logic?

HOLLY

What an opener.

KYLE

I know, right.

HOLLY

Gripped me straight away. As if you had knowledge of the complications of the book that I was reading, whereas all you had done was read the title.

KYLE

You can't teach this kind of flirtation.

Holly leans forward.

HOLLY

Why, yes it is. Have you read it?

KYLE

I've ordered it. I really like his early work on the theory of the impact of nurture on childhood preconceptions.

. . .

HOLLY
It was all quite obvious.

KYLE
Obvious, but brilliant.

HOLLY
Hah! Were you describing yourself, or the book?

KYLE
You tell me.

HOLLY
I can't believe this shit worked on me.

KYLE
But I'm glad it did.

Holly stands.

HOLLY
Well, I've got to go. I'm off to a reading at the book store.

Kyle stands.

KYLE
　No way! Me too. I was just grabbing a coffee to go first.

HOLLY
　You weren't though, were you?

KYLE
　I was praying you wouldn't call my bluff.

HOLLY
　You pig.

KYLE
　Well, it worked.

Kyle walks over to the bedroom. Holly runs in and jumps on him, wrapping her legs around his waist, and running her hands through his hair, kissing him frantically.

KYLE
　Do you do this often?

HOLLY
　Wouldn't you like to know?

. . .

KYLE
Such a mystery.

HOLLY
Got to keep it alive somehow.

KYLE
I'd only known you a few hours.

HOLLY
Yet in those few hours, you knew me very intimately.

Kyle laughs and lays her down on the bed.

KYLE
This is where we did it.

He walks over to the calendar and changes it to 2015. He stands there solemnly, as the lights dim.

He looks over his shoulder at Holly, laying on the bed like a corpse.

KYLE
This is where you did it.

. . .

A few moments, as Kyle sits over Holly's body. Solemn and silent. Holly abruptly stands and changes the calendar to 2011.

HOLLY
I remember that moment.

Kyle stands, upbeat.

KYLE
What moment?

HOLLY
That moment in the Lake District, do you remember? When you fell in the water?

KYLE
What about it?

HOLLY
That was the moment I fell in love with you.
KYLE
Why? I looked like an idiot.

Holly rushes up to him and cups his face sweetly.

HOLLY

But you were *my* idiot.

Kyle lays on the floor and re-enacts falling into the lake.

KYLE
Help, I'm drowning!

HOLLY
So dramatic.

Kyle quickly jumps up, and changes the calendar to 2012, then turns back to Holly excitedly.

KYLE
That time you got that piece of popcorn stuck to your lip in the cinema. It stayed there for the entire movie.

Kyle rearranges the chairs quickly so that they are sat on seats next to each other, as if at the movies.

HOLLY
What?

KYLE
That was when I knew I wanted to spend my life with you.

. . .

HOLLY
  Really?

KYLE
  You looked so cute and helpless.

HOLLY
  Because I had popcorn in my mouth?

KYLE
  Yes. I knew I wanted you forever.

Holly jumps up and changes the calendar to 2013.

HOLLY
  That time....

Kyle jumps up.

KYLE
  That time you cut yourself.

Holly looks to the floor. The tone changes from excitement to sadness.

HOLLY

That time....

KYLE
That was when I knew you were sick.

Holly lays down as if on a hospital bed. Kyle perches beside her, holding her hand.

KYLE
That was when I knew it wasn't fixable. Deep down, I knew.

HOLLY
Oh.

KYLE
I proposed.

HOLLY
You did. After I cut myself?

KYLE
After I knew I wanted to save you.

He stands Holly up and gets on one knee.

. . .

HOLLY
This was hard for me.

KYLE
It was hard for you?

HOLLY
Because I wanted to say yes so much.

KYLE
But you weren't sure, why?

HOLLY
I didn't know if I could put you through everything I knew I would have to put you through.

He stands and kisses her very softly.

KYLE
But I wanted you to put me through it. I wanted to be there.

HOLLY
That's because you still loved me.

KYLE

I never stopped.

HOLLY
Didn't you?

Kyle changes the calendar to 2015, and they both sit together facing the audience. Holly sits back, slumped, at the end of her tether. Kyle clutches onto one of her hands in both of his and leans forward.

KYLE
Doctor, you need to do something. This has been going on for years, and I'm scared. I'm scared of what she might do. Please.

HOLLY
Kyle, they can't help me.

KYLE
Yes, they can. Doctor, please, is there any medication?

HOLLY
They can't help me.

KYLE
They have to!

. . .

Kyle stands. He walks to the side, running his hands through his hair exasperatedly. Holly remains seated, looking at him.

HOLLY

Did you still want to save me then?

KYLE

I did. I did. I just, didn't know how. You wouldn't even try. I pleaded with the Doctors to help you, I begged them. But you didn't. You didn't even move. You just sat there. I begged them to help, and you said nothing.

HOLLY

That's not because I didn't want help.

KYLE

(turning to face her) Then why was it?

HOLLY

Because I knew they couldn't.

Kyle scoffs.

HOLLY

I'd been dealing with this for a lot longer than you had.

. . .

KYLE

I was just so scared I was going to lose you.

Holly goes to change the calendar back, but Kyle quickly grabs her wrist and pulls her back.

KYLE

No, Holly, you can't just rewrite the past.

Holly smiles solemnly as she exits.

Kyle sit, facing the audience, cupping his face in his hands.

KYLE

"You will get better." That's all the Doctors had ever said to her. "Stick with it, you will get better." The other day, my friend, he's a dick, he doesn't quite get how to keep his mouth shut – he asked me, "do you think she's weak for letting depression kill her?" I said no. I think she's strong for staying live as long as she has.

"You will get better." You will get better, what a line. It's an easy line, it just means that they can spin it, and in doing so, dismiss all of what she is feeling. Give it a diagnosis, it suddenly means they aren't real problems any more, she 's just ill, just ill, you will get better, just ill, will get better – did she get fucking better? Did she?

They said they didn't need an autopsy. They knew she was 'ill', they saw all the popped pill packets around her, they didn't even need to check. For all they knew, I killed her. Even in death, her life was dismissed as not even worthy of - …. Sorry. I'm ranting. I just....

Kyle changes the calendar back to 2010, then sits at the table.

Holly enters, full of happiness, putting her arms around him, and kissing him on the cheek.

HOLLY
That was quite a night you gave me last night.

KYLE
Oh yeah?

HOLLY
I could barely walk when I got up this morning, my legs were still shaking.

KYLE
What are you doing today?

HOLLY
That was a risk.

KYLE
What?

. . .

HOLLY

When you asked what I was doing that day. It was a bit clingy. I mean, we had just spent all night shagging.

KYLE

I didn't care. I loved you, then and there.

HOLLY

… Why?

KYLE

Why what?

HOLLY

Why did you love me like you did? Was it because you didn't know I was ill yet? Because being with me was a challenge?

KYLE

It was because when you smiled at me – I felt crazy. I felt mad. Like I was the one who was mental. Not you.

Holly smiles and kisses him.

Exit.

SCENE 3

T*he calendar is on 2012.*

Holly is sat on a chair, down centre stage. Her fists are clenched. She has the television remote in her lap.

She goes to change the channel, then has to press the same button eight times, then presses another button eight times, then stops and clenches her fist.

She goes to change the channel again, touches the button eight times, then taps the remote control on each leg of the chair eight times, then stops and breathes angrily again.

. . .

She goes to change the channel – then stops and screams in frustration.

HOLLY

If I don't tap the same button eight times, then my Mother will die. I feel it, I know it will happen, so I have to tap it. I must tap it. Then I feel like I haven't tapped eight times on the same point of the button, on five on the top bit and three on the bottom, which is awful because those are both odd numbers, whereas eight is a really solid even number, because divided by two is four then by two is two so it is an even even even number, there is no other number except for eighty-eight, but if it made me do it eighty-eight times I swear I will let my Mother die. No I won't. I can't. So I must complete the final three taps at the top and five at the bottom, but then that's bad because they are in segments of odd numbers, so I will repeat that four times to ensure a solid execution of – shit.

She taps the legs of the chair eight times, then eight times again.

HOLLY

If I don't get each leg eight times then I will end up killing Kyle. I don't want to and I know I won't, but I try and resist then I see the knife on the kitchen table and it tells me to do it, so I hide all knives and I stay away from him, but that just makes it worse because it tells me if I stay away from him he will die from other means, maybe he will be mugged or Satan even will come down and slice his heart. So, to save his life, I continue to tap the legs of my chair 8 times each.

. . .

She taps the legs of the chair eight times, then eight times again.

HOLLY

See, I did it again, I did the top of the same leg five times then bottom thre times, so I need to even it up, but solidly even, not twice, but four or eight times. Which means I have to do it another four, but, argh, I don't want to live if I have to live like this!

She stands, screams, and throws the controller across the room. She puts her hands to her face and starts crying.

Kyle enters.

KYLE

Holly? Holly, what's the matter?

HOLLY

And I want to ask him why he moved in with me, knowing he didn't expect this, but I get told if I ask him with those words that I will kill him in my sleep, I've punched him in my sleep before, so I believe this to be true. So I turn to look at him, before it says if I turn then I will die of a heart attack, so I turn the exact same way 8 times until I finally turn to face him and-

She turns to look at him as he places his hands on her arms.

. . .

KYLE

Holly? What's going on? I heard you scream.

HOLLY

I love him. I love him, I really do, I don't want him to die, maybe I should just leave. But I can't leave. If I leave then I will crash my car into a child, that's what it says. And even though I know it's not true, I swear it's not true, I am stuck – here – unable to move. If I move, I will do something and I will have to do it a certain way.

KYLE

Holly, what is it?

HOLLY

I.... want to die.

KYLE

Let's get you some help. Come on, I know we can find someone.

HOLLY

Kyle. I have had five Doctors. None of them gave a shit. They can't help me.

KYLE

But you can't just settle for this life.

. . .

HOLLY

That's why I want to die.

KYLE

Holly, if you died – I would be lost. I can't lose you. I can't.

Holly strokes the side of his face and buries herself in his arms. He strokes her hair.

KYLE

It will be alright, Holly. It will be okay. You will get better.

The lighting abruptly changes to a spot light on the chair. Holly sits in it. Kyle sits in the audience.

HOLLY

A dozen Doctors look at me like I'm not fascinating enough as a case, that I am a burden, that they would far prefer to treat someone with psychosis who can't keep touch with reality, but I know reality, I know the reality of what is wrong with me. OCD. Bipolar Disorder. Depression. What a boring case.

KYLE

How long have you had these thoughts? Do you think you might harm yourself? Why do you worry you will kill people?

HOLLY

I know I won't, I – I know I can't cause someone to die by pressing a button on a remote, but I believe in the chaos theory, somehow it may alter time until... They go through every case study they have. They have a book, a book that says what to do as they cognitive behavioural therapy me, a book that tells them that everyone is the same. That everyone with the same diagnosis will be treated the same. This isn't a broken leg that you can't put in a cast and heal, this is my mind!

KYLE

Are you stupid? What do you waste my time? Do you think you will get better?

HOLLY

No. I know I won't get better. Someday it will beat me. And you will have told yourself you have done all you can. You will keep telling yourself that. You will say it to yourself as you try and sleep. Your wife will convince you of it. No, I'm lying. It won't play on your mind at all. I'm work. As soon as you step foot outside that office, I'm just another statistic.

Kyle re-enters and crouches next to her, taking her hand in his.

KYLE

You will get better.

Holly looks at him, then looks to the floor.

. . .

HOLLY
 Why?

KYLE
 Because you have to, Holly. You have to.

HOLLY
 That isn't a reason.

Exit.

SCENE 4

Calendar changes to 2014. Party ambience. Holly stands, talking to a few (invisible) people, as Kyle does so on the other side of the stage, both holding wine glasses.

HOLLY

Another get together and I stand there and talk. And talk and talk and talk as I have to listen to some more conversations about the weather and where everyone works and then there's my mother. She comes up to me with questions about why I'm not on drugs. She acts like because she's mothered a mental woman she's an expert and starts talking to everyone else in the party. *(in a posh accent)* "People give all the help to the mentally deranged, but never to the parents" she declares with the smug self-authoritarian stance she has whenever she announces any of her revelations. "But what about the mother of the child, she needs some support, where is the support for her, where is the support for her?"

. . .

KYLE

I speak to Holly's father about whatever sports team he supports is doing like it makes any difference and I glance at Holly talking with her overbearing mother and I see that look on her face. She stands there, subjected to that devil's rant and I wonder, should I go over? I just watch her for a little bit, never knowing whether it's best to leave her be or play the hero.

HOLLY

"I had to witness her cuts on her arms when she was a child, that kind of thing is traumatic for me, oh where is that damn boy with my drink". She goes from the dreadful recollection of her daughter self-harming to the anger of her son not bringing over her beverage to allow her to fuel her alcoholic brain within the same sentence, dismissing yet again that other people's problems may be significant.

KYLE

I swear her mother's blood type is vodka. I can see she's getting drunk again, and acting like she is the messiah. I end the conversation with her father and slowly make my way for support.

HOLLY

She notices Kyle and starts involving him in her self-holy perspective "oh Kyle, shouldn't you get support to, it can't be easy living with a mental woman, I don't know why you do it, I had no choice." She declares.

. . .

KYLE

Well actually, I'm quite happy to support her anyway I can.

HOLLY

"Oh my dear boy, don't get so defensive, I didn't mean to challenge you as a man, I know you must be here for a reason, but you don't know the promiscuity that is involved in the manic phases of her bipolar disorder, I mean she was arranging her ceiling tiles into sequences of eight for most of her adolescence."

KYLE

Holly, maybe we should think about leaving.

HOLLY

How dare he challenge her, she thinks. She couldn't stand him anyway. Never mind the fact that he takes care of her daughter, it's the fact that his job is low paid that she focusses on. That must be the reason he's there, to leach of my inheritance when she dies. A point at which I am sure that we will dance on her carcass. Then I remember how much I believe she will die, so I start touching the same part of my wine glass in sequences of eight, then sipping it, drowning out her voice.

KYLE

Or maybe we should go get a drink.

HOLLY

"Kyle, don't be such a drip. She has no reason to be depressed, she's had everything she has ever wanted, why be depressed, why obsess, why think you are anything but blessed, I mean really my dear. Did you know she used to carry broken glass in her bag at school so she could cut herself in the toilet?" She observes, making hilarity out of my teenage predicament. Making hilarity out of the fact that I did not have a childhood. "I mean, I did everything I could to make her happy but she was just insistent"

KYLE
Please, let's just go-

HOLLY
"Kyle, you weak man"

KYLE
I mean, seriously

HOLLY
"Why don't you just leave-"

KYLE
(*shouts*) STOP!

Party ambience abruptly stops.

. . .

KYLE

Enough! You stupid old bag. Why don't you try spending one minute in her shoes. You think she has a choice? You think this is what she wanted? Maybe she did have a reason to be unhappy, maybe it was you. If you are so ashamed of what she has become, maybe you should look at yourself you batty old mare!

Silence.

HOLLY

Everyone in the party has stopped talking. Everyone has turned and stared. My mother just looks at him, not shocked nor taken aback – just full of awe at this urchin her daughter has allowed into their family home.

KYLE

I will be in the car.

HOLLY

My father comes over and suggests that maybe he should take my mother out for a breather.

Kyle exits.

HOLLY

She smiles. Like she won. Like she got the better of him. I

just look at her and say. "Don't worry, Mother. You will get better."

She places her wine glass on the table and turns to the audience.

HOLLY
She won't.

Exit.

SCENE 5

Kyle and Holly enter their bedroom and start getting changed, not interacting. Uncomfortable silence ensues. They both make the bed together, again in silence.

Kyle pauses and exhales.

KYLE
Holly.

HOLLY
Mm?

KYLE
Your Mum was well out of order.

. . .

HOLLY
I don't want to talk about it.

KYLE
Don't you need to?

HOLLY
Kyle, I – I just. I'm fed up.

KYLE
I know you are.

HOLLY
No, really, I am just – fed up.

Kyle smiles. He walks over to her. He kisses her.

He starts kissing her neck. Holly looks very uncomfortable.

He goes to remove his top.

HOLLY
Stop.

Kyle freezes. Holly turns to the audience.

. . .

HOLLY

This is the point I dread. I – I know he wants to have sex. And I know how long it has been. I know I should. I know if I say no, he will be understanding, it's just – he has given this all up for me.

Kyle unfreezes and hastily removes his top off. He puts his arms around her waist from behind, and continues to kiss her neck. Holly faces the audience.

HOLLY

Every time he kisses me, it comes back. If he kisses the side of my neck, he has to do it a certain number of times in the same point, and when he doesn't, it stresses me out, but I can't tell him. This is one of life's greatest activities, we did it daily at the beginning, it's now, just...

She peals away, turns, and looks at him.

KYLE

What is it?

HOLLY

How can I answer that question? How can I tell him I count how many times he penetrates me to make sure it is a multiple of eight? That I can't have an orgasm because the whole thing is just one big episode of anxiety and I'm concentrating too much on –

Holly leans her forehead against Kyle's.

KYLE
What is it, Holly? Don't you want to?

HOLLY
Of course I want to.

KYLE
Then come on. Just relax.

HOLLY
Just relax! A part of me is angry that he just said it to me, then I remember he doesn't know. He can't know what is going on in my mind. What can I tell him?

KYLE
What?

HOLLY
I'm not in the mood.

Kyle pulls away.

. . .

HOLLY

I am in the mood. I am so in the mood. I am always in the mood, and I want him so bad. Just as bad as he wants me, it's just... I know it will take hours to get to sleep. And I need to be awake for work in the morning. Maybe I could use that excuse. Or a headache – no that hasn't worked since he found that article about how sex cures a headache.

KYLE

Are you ever in the mood, Holly? I don't want to pressure you into anything, I just-

He gazes at her for a few moments.

HOLLY

I'm sorry.

He gets into bed.

Holly is left standing there.

HOLLY

And it's amazing. Amazing how I can have someone who loves me so much and supports me so much, but in one moment – can make me feel so alone.

She climbs into bed, turns, and looks at him.

. . .

HOLLY
I love you.

Silence.

HOLLY
He's already asleep. I guess I'll have to cry on my own.

Exit.

SCENE 6

Upbeat jazzy music. The calendar is turned to 2013.

Kyle jumps onto the stage, with an open shirt over a pair of boxers. With the beats of the music, he gleefully puts on some trousers. He freezes in a moment of silence during a momentary pause within the beats of the music, then when the beats return, he gleefully does up his shirt. He dances to the music in a similar vein until he is smartly dressed.

The music changes to the wedding march. Kyle stands down centre stage. Holly walks from up stage, as if walking down the aisle. As she reaches Kyle, they turn to face each other.

HOLLY
    I do.

. . .

KYLE

I do.

They kiss. Inspiration music.

Holly sits down. Kyle stands forward, as if it is the reception, and he is giving the speech.

KYLE

My best men – I couldn't have done it without you. You had my back and gave me a hell of a send-off. Then, my wife. I thought I had prepared myself for today. I thought I had myself mentally ready. But when I saw you coming down the aisle – I was taken aback. I couldn't speak. Never, have I seen anything so beautiful, in all my life. Ladies and gentlemen, please raise your glass, to my wife.

Kyle raises his glasses.

KYLE

And now, we must turn our attention to absent family and friends.

Kyle freezes. The music abruptly ends.

. . .

Holly stands, walks over to the calendar, changes it to 2015, and exits.

Kyle continues his speech, but it has now become his funeral speech.

KYLE
I, er... I thought I had prepared myself for this. But... Many people know my Holly had been ill for a while. I just...

He looks down, trying to compose himself. He takes a few moments.

KYLE
My Holly was strong. She was the strongest person I know. This day isn't about her weakness as a person, but the strength of her illness. She made my life worth living. She made my life...

Kyle steps down and sits on a seat, drinking from a beer can. He loosens his shirt and tie.

KYLE
I'm sat in the corner, surveying the room. Half the people I don't recognise. Once I managed to pin a few to their Facebook profile pictures, I realise they are friends who haven't seen Holly for, like, five years. Haven't seen her for 5 years – and they turn up to her funeral. If they really cared, why didn't they show her when she was alive. Why didn't they visit when –

. . .

He abruptly stops himself, and stands.

KYLE

A group of strangers come up to me to offer their condolences. I nod and smile, nod and smile, nod and smile. I know it's hard to decide whether you should approach the widower or not, but bear in mind you fair weathered friends, I did not come here for you. I did not come here to hear how sorry you are. They say they are sorry. I say "... for what?" Did you kill her? Did you cause her death? Then what the fuck are you sorry for?

Kyle walks toward the exit, then pauses.

KYLE

The whole time, it just went around my head and around my head, the same question. Could I have stopped this?

Exit.

SCENE 7

The calendar is changed to 2014, possibly as Kyle exits the stage from the previous scene.

Holly sits on a single chair in the middle of the stage.

HOLLY

Doctor what's-his-name and that Doctor-with-a-moustache pop into the room to offer their observations. They don't say anything, but they write a lot. They write and write and write.

Kyle enters, as the Doctor.

KYLE

My name is Doctor-who-doesn't-give-a-shit. I have been

conferring with Doctor-with-a-moustache and we are considering whether to have you sectioned.

HOLLY

If I'm sectioned, you will take me away from my job and my career. You will take me away from my husband, the only one thing that keeps me going.

KYLE

Holly, we are just trying to consider what is in your best interests.

HOLLY

That's a joke.

KYLE

Holly, do you think you might harm yourself?

HOLLY

Will you section me if I say yes?

KYLE

Are you scared of being alone?

HOLLY

Aren't you?

. . .

KYLE
Maybe we should increase your medication.

HOLLY
No, please... It doesn't help... It just numbs me...

KYLE
Holly, do you want to get better?

Holly looks up, full of anger.

Kyle exits.

HOLLY
Do I want to get better?

Kyle re-enters as Kyle, on the phone.

KYLE
Yeah. Yeah, yeah, that's great. Thank you so much. No, thank you, all the best.

He hangs up and turns to Holly.

KYLE

That was work, I – I've just been promoted. I am now regional supervisor.

Holly says nothing, facing away.

KYLE
Holly, this is great news for me, aren't you excited?

HOLLY
(blankly) Congratulations.

KYLE
What? You're not happy for me?

HOLLY
Sure.

KYLE
Holly, I know you aren't at your best, but the least you could do is give me a heartfelt well done.

He pours himself a drink.

HOLLY
Well done.

. . .

Silence.

KYLE
Well that's mature.

HOLLY
What?

KYLE
This is my dream, Holly. This is all I've ever wanted. Why aren't you happy for me?

Holly stands, and walks over to the other side of the stage.

HOLLY
I am happy for you, Kyle.

KYLE
Then why can't you look happy?

HOLLY
Because it's not that simple!

KYLE
Yes it is! Even the most clinically depressed could at least

give their boyfriend a pat on the back when they get a promotion?

Holly glares at him, spitefully. She pats his back sarcastically.

HOLLY
Well done Kyle, have a huge pat on the back, here you go, you earned it. Well done, Kyle, well done. Now you can spend more time there, away from me. Maybe you can fuck your secretary, I bet she is in full mental health.

KYLE
You're being unfair, Holly.

HOLLY
Am I?

KYLE
Yes, you are!

He toward her, goes to touch her, then backs off.

KYLE
If I didn't think that you could do whatever you wanted to do, then why would I have stuck with you for so long? I tell you all the time, you will get better, I don't just say that as an aww, here's a pat on the head for feeling down, I say that

because I know you, and I know you're strong. But can't you, for one minute, just one minute, break out of it to let me know that I have done well when I want to share my life with you. Because I do want to share my life with you and I, I will not – I will not, for one minute pretend that I don't.

Holly shakes her head, facing away.

KYLE
But with all this support I give you, couldn't you just give me one single ounce of what I have given you. Just one. Just something that means you support me.

Holly turns slightly toward him and half smiles.

HOLLY
I guess. I know.

Kyle smiles at her.

KYLE
Just for one moment, Holly. Put all your problems on hold.

Pause. Holly grows angry, backing away.

HOLLY

What did you just say?

KYLE

What?

HOLLY

You want me to put all my problems on hold?

KYLE

Holly, that's not what I meant.

HOLLY

How do I put it on hold, huh! How do I put it on hold, Kyle? Oh, I know, today I won't have OCD. Today I won't believe I'm going to die every time I want to move. Perhaps I will just snap out of feeling depressed too, bipolar disorder is so easy to snap out of.

KYLE

Holly -

HOLLY

No, don't say my name Kyle, of course, this is all about you – what's up with you today, huh? Let's put my OCD on hold and find out?

KYLE

Holly. I have supported you the whole way. Don't do this.

HOLLY
Do what?

KYLE
Act so irrationally! You won't find anyone else who will deal with your issues like I have.

Long uncomfortable silence.

HOLLY
You're right, I won't. Because I'm so hard to deal with.

KYLE
That's not what I meant.

HOLLY
Yes, Kyle. It is.

Holly exits.

Kyle is left standing there.

. . .

He walks over to the bed. He sits down on the edge of it, sadly. He takes a good few moments of contemplation.

KYLE

I was sat in a bar, nursing a bottle of lager. She came and spoke to me. It was so easy. Compared to what I'm used to, it was so, so easy. She asked me where I worked, I told her about my promotion, she shook my hand. She looked me in the eye, said congratulations, and shook my hand. She didn't even know me. She tossed her hair over her shoulder and it looked so cute, she bought me another beer, and another...

I didn't love her. I couldn't, I was already in love. But I wanted her. Not because I was attracted to her. She was attractive and I was attracted, don't get me wrong. It was because she wanted me. And she gave me... everything.

Holly never needs to know. Holly doesn't need to know.

Exit.

SCENE 8

Calendar is changed to 2015.

Holly sits alone, on a chair. Music starts – repetitive, mechanical music.

Holly taps each leg of the chair in a sequence to the music. She does this again, and again, and again.

The music stops and Holly sits still for a second, rocking back and forth, grabbing her hair, frustrated.

The music suddenly starts again. Holly repeating another obsessive sequence of activities, this time tapping different things in the room, such as the bed, walls and chairs in a repetitive motion. She does this again, and again, and again.

Music stops again. Holly stands there, panting, out of breath, exasperated.

The music immediately restarts. This time it is going faster, and Holly must repeat a sequence involving props of the stage, as well as the floor and walking up and off the stage. She repeats this to the music, as it gets faster and faster, again, and again, and again.

Music stops. Holly lets out a scream.

HOLLY
Stop!

The music barely lets her any time to stop until it restarts again and she must continue repeating the sequence, getting too fast to bear, repeating again, and again, and again.

The music abruptly ends as Holly screams, and kicks the chair across the stage. She walks back and forth, grabbing her hair and breathing heavily, at her wit's end.

HOLLY
(*screaming*) Fuck off! Fuck off fuck off fuck off fuck off!

. . .

She trashes the room in anger, throwing the table over, ripping paper, kicking beer cans away, destroying all props.

HOLLY
(*screaming as she trashes the room*) Leave me alone! Just leave me alone! Go away!

Holly falls to her knees.

She kneels for a few moments, breathing heavily. She sobs.

HOLLY
Why? Why are you doing this to me? You are voices in my head, thoughts in my head, you are me. So why are you bullying me? And why can't I control you? And why do I believe you! I know I won't kill anyone, I won't die, I won't, I know, so why do I believe you!

She looks around at the room that she has destroyed.

HOLLY
This is my head. This room, the state of the room, this is my head. There is not a moment when you are not screaming at me, why will you not just stop screaming at me! How am I supposed to talk to a psychiatrist about you, they have studied you, they have never been you. They have never had their head scream, they have never known why we do this, they have

never – cried themselves to sleep because they just want, to sleep, and for it all to stop.

She breaks down completely.

HOLLY

I have even had conversations with you. I have literally spoken to you, in my mind, and asked you, why do you bully me. If I was had a leg in a cast, people could see what is wrong with me, people could know what to do to help me, but I tell people I have OCD, yet they still expect me to do everything, to work as a normal person, but I am not normal, I have never been normal. Normal people do not have conversations with voices in their head that tell them they will die if they don't have the television on an even fucking channel, that is not normal, I am not normal.

She weeps into her hands.

HOLLY

You have driven me to this. You, have driven me to this. You, have killed me. Not me. You. You cannot be a part of me. Maybe you're the voice of God, or maybe you're the voice of a demon inside me, but you cannot be me.

She stands, and walks over to a bag, withdrawing boxes of medication and a bottle of wine. She stares at them.

. . .

HOLLY

Fluoxetine Hydrochloride, trade name Prozac. 20mg is normal does. I take sixty a day. Sertraline, another antidepressant. And a bottle of red wine. Everything I have.

She holds it all tightly in her hands, closes her eye,s and tries to gather herself.

HOLLY

Is this what it takes to shut you up? Is this what it takes? You tell me not to take it, you tell me what will happen if I do. But this, for the first time in my life, is when I don't listen to you. Because after this, you are quiet.

She throws the medication on the floor.

Holly walks over to the calendar and turns the year from 2015 to a black card. She pauses at this position of the stage.

Kyle enters, picks up the chair, sits down and looks at her.

Silence.

HOLLY

You were my last hope.

. . .

KYLE

You didn't need hope, you needed help.

HOLLY

(shakes her head) You're wrong.

KYLE

What is it that made you give up, after you survived this long?

HOLLY

What is it that made me survive this long, after I'd already given up?

Pause.

KYLE

I love you.

HOLLY

I loved you.

KYLE

You would have gotten better.

HOLLY

You are so naive.

Kyle leans forward.

KYLE
What should I tell your Mum?

HOLLY
Tell her... Whatever she wants to hear.

KYLE
She'll blame me.

HOLLY
I don't care.

Holly walks over to him, and strokes her hands down the side of his face. He rests his head against her belly and puts his arms around her.

He quietly sobs.

KYLE
Is this real?

. . .

Holly shrugs.

He lifts his head to look at her.

HOLLY
This is what I wanted.

KYLE
You keep telling yourself that.

HOLLY
This is the only way.

Kyle stands up and looks at her, taking a few moments, just looking in her eyes.

KYLE
I blame myself.

Holly smiles.

HOLLY
There is nothing I can do about that now.

KYLE

You remember when I met you?

HOLLY
I noticed your eyes.

KYLE
I noticed your smile.

HOLLY
I noticed your hair.

KYLE
I noticed your tits.

They lean their foreheads on each other, giggle, before moving into a kiss. The kiss becomes passionate. Just as it starts to become passionate, Holly rips away and stands back. Kyle stays standing there, with his eyes closed.

Holly exits.

Lights dim as Kyle turns to the audience.

He goes to say something, then doesn't.

. . .

He picks up a black bin bag and starts cleaning up the mess Holly had left, picking up ripped paper and prescription boxes.

He puts the chairs and tables back.

He makes the bed.

Once the stage is tidied up again, he walks to front centre stage.

He goes to speak – then doesn't.

He walks over to the calendar in the corner of the stage. He looks at it solemnly for a few moments. He flips the date back to 2011.

Holly enters cheerfully, walks up to him, and flings her arms around him.

HOLLY
Hey, what are you doing here? The weather is ace outside.

He turns to faces her.

KYLE
Do you love me, Holly?

. . .

HOLLY
Of course I do, silly.

She kisses him on the cheek.

HOLLY
Now come on.

He pulls her back by the hand and embraces her.

KYLE
You are perfect. You know that, right?

HOLLY
Okay, don't be silly.

KYLE
No, I mean it – you are perfect.

He lifts her face up and gives her a long, gentle kiss.

She leans back and looks at him, her eyes full of love.

KYLE
Don't ever leave me.

. . .

HOLLY
　I won't. I promise.

She stands back and grabs his hand.

HOLLY
　Now come on outside, it's so sunny.

KYLE
　I'll be there in a minute.

HOLLY
　Okay, don't be long.

She kisses him on the cheek and exits.

Kyle walks slowly toward the exit, contemplating.

He turns around, looks at the audience momentarily, then switches the light switch off.

Exit.

AFTERWORD

Message from the author:

This play has been based on my personal experience of having OCD and bipolar disorder. I hope if you have experienced such trials, that this play has given you comfort in being able to relate.

I am primarily a horror and thriller writer, and if you are interested in my novels, you can find more at **www.rickwoodwriter.com**

All the best,
    Rick

www.ingramcontent.com/pod-product-compliance
Lightning Source LLC
LaVergne TN
LVHW090038080526
838202LV00046B/3861